A Kid Lit Science Book

Astro-Tot

The SOLAR SYSTEM

by
Julia Stilchen

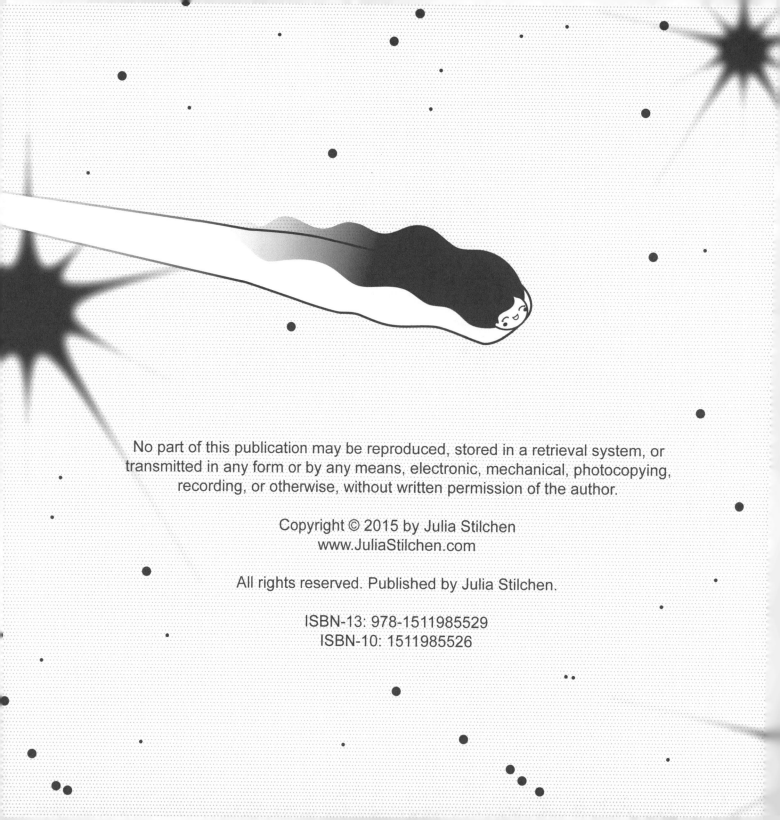

Copyright © 2015 by Julia Stilchen
www.JuliaStilchen.com

All rights reserved. Published by Julia Stilchen.

ISBN-13: 978-1511985529
ISBN-10: 1511985526

To Jovan, Serenity, my husband,
family and friends, and all the
stargazers around the world!

Milky Way

Sun

Mercury

Venus

Earth

Jupiter

Saturn

Uranus

Neptune

Pluto

Haumea

Makemake

AUTHOR NOTE

Hi There! Thank you for reading my book. It is a joy to have the opportunity to create children's books to share among family, friends, and the rest of the world.

I am inspired and dedicated to produce quality books. I hope that you enjoyed reading and if you have the time, I'd love if you could leave an honest review for my book. It helps me out greatly to get my book out into the world as an Indie Author.

I'd also enjoy hearing back from my readers with any comments, questions or feedback on how I could improve my books. You can email me at stilchenbooks@gmail.com

Thank you again and Happy Reading!

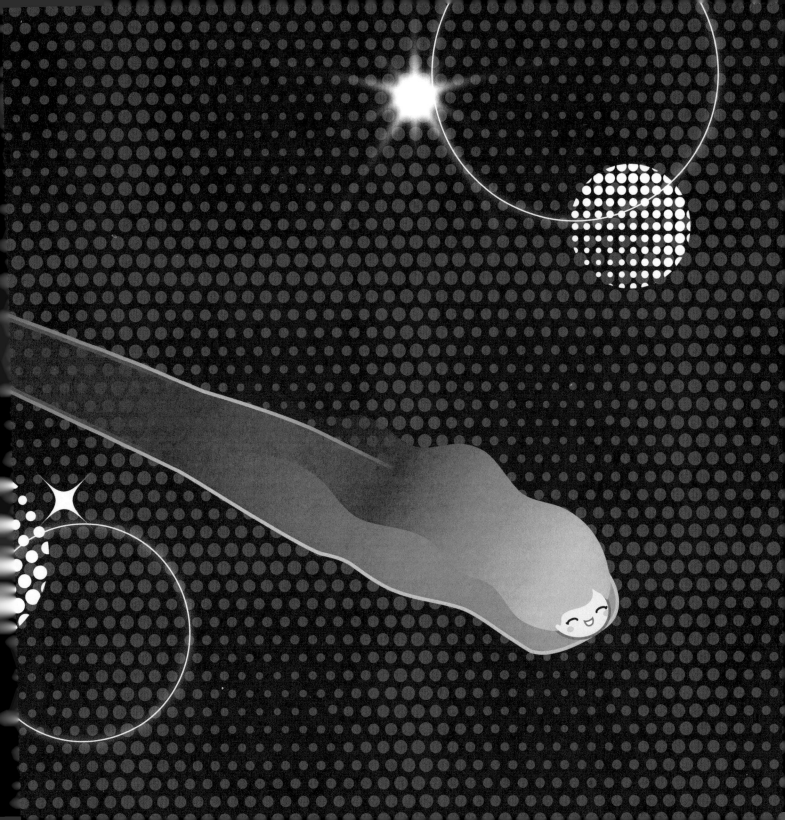

40647524R00022

Made in the USA
Middletown, DE
18 February 2017